9-1-1 Super Emergency

By

Joel M. Caplan

New Jersey
USA

Copyright © 2014 by Joel M. Caplan

All rights reserved. No part of this book may be reproduced in any manner without written permission by the copyright holder. Original clipart images were obtained from openclipart.org.

Produced by Joel M. Caplan:
Specializing in consulting, speaking and training to inform policy and practice decisions relating to safety and security at the local, national and international levels. Visit www.joelcaplan.com for more information and additional books for children.

About this book: Teaches toddlers and young children how to recognize an emergency and call 9-1-1 for help. This exciting picture storybook is excellent for early childhood education and community programming focused on public safety.

This book is dedicated to
public safety dispatchers,
first responders, and everyone who
is prepared to be a hero everyday
by knowing how to recognize an
emergency and call 9-1-1.

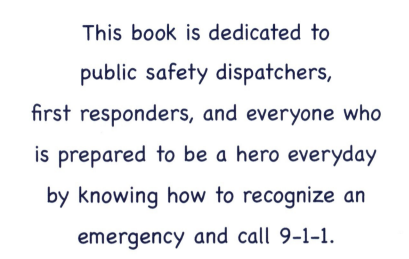

If you know your ABCs and your 123s, then YOU can be a hero in emergencies!

What is an emergency?

An **emergency** is when you need a police officer, firefighter or ambulance for **help right away.**

If you are lost or scared and alone, that's also an emergency!

Medical

Allergic Reaction

Choking • Drowning

Hear Yelling for "Help"
Crime • Car Crash

"Won't Wake Up" • Not Breathing
If in Doubt, Call

There are **many kinds of** emergencies.

When they happen, do YOU know what to do?

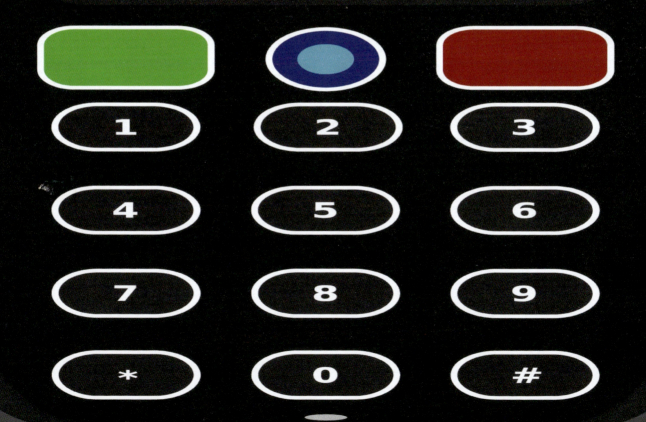

The phone will start to ring.

RING. R-I-I-NG. R-I-I-I-NG.

Someone will answer: "9-1-1, where's your emergency?"

Talk to the person on the phone.

They are superheroes too!

Answer their **questions** and do what they tell you.

9-1-1 is not a game.

And it's definitely not for fun.

Only for emergencies dial 9-1-1.

Now when you notice an emergency
you know exactly what to do.
Quickly **tell an adult** or **call 9-1-1**
and be a **superhero to the rescue!**

Adults: Teach children how to use your landline and cellular phones to dial 9-1-1. Teach other options too for people who are hearing or speech impaired. For cell phones, train children to press 9-1-1 and then the "send" button. Do not practice by calling 9-1-1 for real. Even cell phones without active service can be used to call 9-1-1 (so they aren't toys). Be sure children know they don't need money to call 9-1-1 from a pay phone. Teach nine-one-one, not nine-eleven; there is no eleven button on phones. Explain to children that they should first tell a nearby trusted adult if they notice an emergency. Someone like father, mother, sister, brother, grandma, grandpa, teacher, babysitter, etc. If they cannot find an adult, then use a phone to call 9-1-1. If there is a fire or other hazard, get to a safe place first. If children are on the phone and feel in danger, teach them to go to a safe place without hanging-up the phone. Do not hang-up the phone until the 9-1-1 operator says to. If you or a close friend or family member has a known medical condition that may require emergency treatment (such as diabetes, epilepsy, etc.), teach your child about it (signs/symptoms) and what to do in an emergency situation. Teach children how to say their first and last names. Note that places outside of the United States may use other numbers for emergencies.

Build Confidence: Practice Calling 9-1-1

Practice with both landlines (unplugged) and cell phones (batteries out). Do not practice by calling 9-1-1 for real. Practice different types of scenarios.

Practice Script (using a disconnected phone):

Child: [Dials 9-1-1]

Ring, Ring...

Operator: *"9-1-1, where's your emergency?"* Most operators are trained to ask "where" first, then "what".

Child: The child should start with *"I need help"* then state the problem and where it is located.

Operator: *"OK. I am going to get you help. What is your name?"* The operator will likely talk to the child by name. This helps to calm the situation and allows for more clear and detailed answers to important follow-up questions.

Child: [states name] (Full name if possible)

Operator: [repeats child's name] "Do not hang up. Stay on the phone with me. Help is on the way."

Notes: The above script is standard. The operator may ask additional questions, depending on the type of emergency. E.g., "Are you OK?" "How old are you?" "Is the person still around?" "What did the person look like?" The operator may also instruct the child to listen for sirens or to say when he/she sees or hears a first responder approaching.

Young Children Really Can (And Do) Save Lives by Calling 9-1-1

On August 2, 2002, Special Officer Class II/Communication Operator Joel Caplan answered a 9-1-1 call from a 7-year-old boy who stated that he could not awaken his mother. Caplan handled this life-threatening situation with professionalism and compassion and insured that the proper care was obtained for both the mother and young son. Additionally, Caplan's interaction with the young boy at the Cape May Police Department displayed kindness and concern for the boy's general well being during this traumatic event. Caplan is a credit to this Department and the law enforcement community.

Diane M. Sorantino — Chief of Police
Robert F. Sheehan, Jr. — Lieutenant
Jean K. Westlund — Administrative Clerk

DEPARTMENT OF POLICE
CITY OF CAPE MAY
National Historic Landmark

643 Washington Street
Cape May, New Jersey 08204
609-884-9500 Fax: 609-884-9589

CAPE MAY POLICE DEPARTMENT
PERFORMANCE NOTICE

Date: August 3, 2002
Name: Joel Caplan
Rank: Special Officer Class II/Communication Operator

Commendation: __XX__ Appraisal: ____ Counseling: ____ Warning: ____

Statement of Circumstances

On August 2, 2002, Special Officer Class II/Communication Operator Joel Caplan answered a 9-1-1 call from a 7-year-old boy who stated that he could not awaken his mother. Caplan handled this life-threatening situation with professionalism and compassion and insured that the proper care was obtained for both the mother and young son. Additionally, Caplan's interaction with the young boy at the Cape May Police Department displayed kindness and concern for the boy's general well being during this traumatic event. Caplan is a credit to this Department and the law enforcement community.

Subject's Signature Lieutenant Robert Sheehan

About the Author

Joel M. Caplan, Ph.D. is an Associate Professor at Rutgers University School of Criminal Justice and Deputy Director of the Rutgers Center on Public Security. He is an internationally recognized public safety scholar with professional experience as a police officer, 9-1-1 dispatcher, and Emergency Medical Technician (EMT). As a Basic Life Support (BLS) instructor for the American Heart Association, he regularly teaches CPR to people of all ages. Joel is a proud father and the author of several books for children, including *Strangers Can Hurt* which teaches toddlers how to judge risks and avoid harm. He presents to community groups and at various professional conferences and public safety agencies around the world (www.joelcaplan.com).

Find the 9s and 1s

9 2 4 3 7 6 5 8 0 9 0 8 7 6 4 3 5 2 9 6 5 4
7 8 0 3 2 0 9 2 4 3 5 6 8 7 0 9 8 7 6 5 4 3
9 0 8 7 6 2 3 4 5 9 2 3 4 5 7 8 6 0 1 4 2 5
3 7 6 8 0 1 3 2 6 5 4 7 8 0 1 3 2 4 5 7 8 0
1 3 2 4 6 5 4 8 7 1 5 4 6 7 3 5 4 6 9 8 5 7 6
4 3 7 5 1 3 1 5 7 6 4 8 9 0 7 8 6 4 5 1 7 5 6
9 1 1 4 3 6 7 8 6 5 2 7 8 0 1 3 2 4 5 7 6 8 0
1 3 2 4 6 5 4 8 7 1 3 4 5 7 8 6 0 9 4 2 5 3 7
6 8 0 9 3 2 6 5 4 7 8 0 1 3 2 4 5 7 6 8 0 1 3
2 5 7 6 2 3 4 5 9 2 9 2 4 3 7 6 5 8 0 9 0 8
7 6 4 4 3 6 5 4 7 8 0 7 8 6 4 5 1 7 5 6 9 1 1

Color the super phone. Where do the numbers go?

Made in the USA
San Bernardino, CA
11 September 2014